A Service D

PAWSITIVELY DAX

by Mike Dickerson

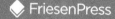

One Printers Way
Altona, MB R0G 0B0
Canada

www.friesenpress.com

Copyright © 2022 by Mike Dickerson
First Edition — 2022

All rights reserved.

ISBN
978-1-03-913108-8 (Hardcover)
978-1-03-913107-1 (Paperback)
978-1-03-913109-5 (eBook)

1. JUVENILE NONFICTION, ANIMALS, DOGS

Distributed to the trade by The Ingram Book Company

PAWSITIVELY DAX

Hi, I'm Dax.

It's so very nice to meet you! I'm from a small town near Kansas City, Missouri. I've just found out I get to be a Service Dog when I'm older. That means I will be like a personal assistant for someone. I will help when they need it, like by carrying groceries or helping them use stairs and elevators. Do you know any Service Dogs?

Oh! It's official now: I get to go to school with my best pal, Mike!

Our teacher's name is Mrs. Gloria. She will be teaching us the basics of being a Service Dog. I'm going to be a Veterans Affairs Service Dog. But did you know that all dogs can train to behave better? To help, there is a test called the "Good Citizen Canine Test."

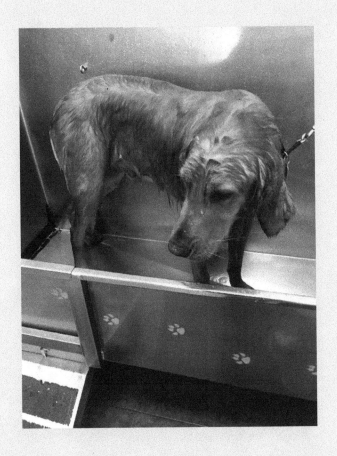

Who doesn't love a good spa day after a long day of school
and meeting new friends, all while traveling around town?

I learned that dogs know around four hundred words of human language.

My best pal, Mike, doesn't think he knows four hundred words.
Hey, could you pass that scented puppy shampoo over here?
The baby powder scent is my favorite.

Well, after months of training, learning, and memorizing
my commands and cues with my best pal, Mike,

I've grown into a 138-pound, fully-trained Service Dog.

My super size has also given me super pawsitivity
and super personality. I promise to do my best.

I have a place I like to call the Training Circle. My best pal, Mike, and I catch as many sunrises and sunsets as we can while training with hand signals and commands.

I pawsitively love to exercise!

There is something pawsitively awesome about
the wind in my face when I'm traveling.

Sometimes I like to sing along to the radio.

Remember to ask before interacting with a Service Dog.
When my gear is on, I'm working with my best pal. Your dog wants
to give you their full attention. Service Dogs are the same way.
Have you ever seen a Service Dog at the store?"
Maybe at the airport or your school?

Have you ever been on an airplane?

I get the best naps in when I fly.

I've never met an airline employee I didn't like. I also have never run across a rude passenger. My best pal, Mike, says it is because I am always kind and set a pawsitive example.

Bringing pawsitivity to hospitals, schools, churches, and long-term care facilities has helped me make so many new friends.

It's nice just to make someone's day a little better.

Where do you go to visit your friends and make their days better?

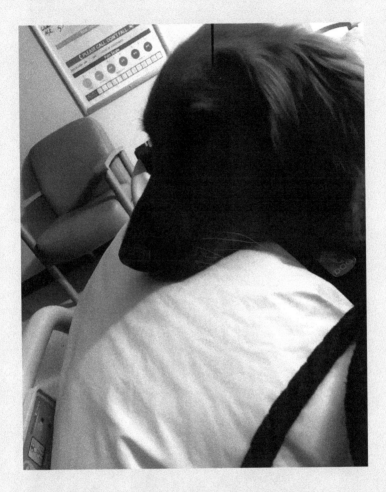

Visiting families and letting them know it's going to be okay is tougher on some days than others. But I remind the people I get the chance to meet that there is always hope, even when I'm just offering a pillow, or pawsitively offering to *be* a pillow for a while.

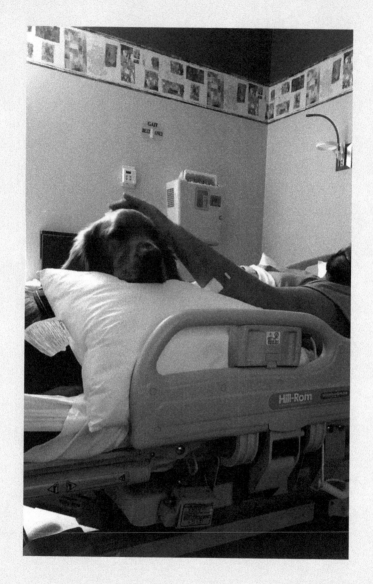

Sometimes I let my pawsitivity help out doctors and nurses.
They do their best to take care of their patients. Hang in there.
There's no need to be a cranky critter.

Being a pawsitively super-sized Service Dog is such a great way of life—just not on an empty stomach.

Service Dogs have special manners.

It's not polite for us to accept food from others or even suggest eating outside our routines. But that doesn't mean that we go without. We just like our downtime without gear so we can let our hair down a bit. It helps us bond with our special pals too.

My favorite treat in the world is a Puppuccino.

I have some drive-thru friends that help me through a day with a pawsitively wonderful cup of awesomeness! And it doesn't hurt being large enough to meet my friends halfway through the truck window.

Do you ever play hide-and-seek? When people find me hiding in the gear it brings out smiles from ear to ear.

I pawsitively love to smile!

Oh, fall and winter!

Playing in the leaves and making snow angels leaves me pawsitively speechless. I love fresh, cool air flowing through my golden hair. Have you ever made a snow angel?

The holidays are always pawsitively exciting.

It means more time with my family and friends to tell them all about my adventures. This is my little brother, Remi. My best pal, Mike, keeps getting his name wrong calling him "Handful," but his name really is Remi.

Do you have a Christmas sweater? I pawsitively need to look good when I go see Santa. Remi looks great in his sweater.

We get to see Santa soon.

I'm going to ask for a Puppuccino for Remi and myself.

Santa says I've been a very good Service Dog.

He has a special present for me this year as a reward for my
pawsitivity. Are you being pawsitive? What are some things you
do during the holidays? Do you go see Santa too? I'm *so excited!*
Santa brings out our smiles.

While minding my own business, waiting for Santa
and being curious about what he is bringing,

I volunteer to judge the gingerbread houses.

I'm the best choice because I can see above tables and counters
with my height and my super-sized pawsitivity. Okay, it smells too
good not to take a bite. *Shh*—don't tell my best pal, Mike.

Oh! Santa gave me *pawsitively supercharged reindeer antlers!*

I'm an honorary reindeer!

Now I get to visit more hospitals, schools, and churches, to make even *more* new friends, *and* help Santa. Being a great Service Dog all year round sure has made a difference. Have you ever met a reindeer? Or an honorary one?

I sure do like my responsibilities and opportunities as a Service Dog.

Pawsitive adventures with a pawsitive personality is something that's always worth teaching others, like my little brother, Remi. Who do you share your pawsitive adventures with?

No, no, Remi! I said,

"Let's be a pawsitive boy!"

Not "Pawsitively take my toy!" Now *give that back!* I think my brother, Remi, wants his own adventure book. I'm starting to understand that name, "Handful," that my best pal, Mike, calls him.

Each day is a new adventure for my super pawsitive personality. Do you ever get so excited to go and see what things are in store for you?

Tell me something pawsitive you get to do!

Who do you get to do that with?

Just a quick reminder: always ask before petting.

Remember that a Service Dog in his gear has a set of manners and a diet to follow. It helps us be pawsitive and do our best for our best pals. If you know a dog that would like to learn more, try the Good Citizen Canine Test. Thank you for helping me.

No matter where you travel in the world,

you can be a pawsitively wonderful blessing to others.

Make as many friends as you can and enjoy each day knowing you can make a difference. Oh, and don't forget to catch a sunrise or sunset.

This has been such a fun adventure.

Thank you so much for being my pawsitively wonderful new friend.
I hope we get a chance to do this again soon. Let's put some good
in the world one paw at a time. I'll see you soon.

**Believe
there is
good in the
world**

CPSIA information can be obtained
at www.ICGtesting.com
Printed in the USA
BVHW061549090222
628492BV00017B/1782